Don't Touch My Tutu

or

The Perilous Decline
of Cora Sline *

A Comedy in Two Acts

By

EDDIE COPE

*You may choose either title for your performance

I. E. CLARK PUBLICATIONS
PO Box 246, Schulenburg, TX 78956-0246
Phone (979)743-3232 ** FAX (979)743-4765
E-mail: ieclark@cvtv.net

THE PERILOUS DECLINE OF CORA SLINE

Characters

PA CLEANLIVIN, owner of a restaurant
MA CLEANLIVIN, his wife
SONNY CLEANLIVIN, their son
COLONEL QUESTUS QUANTRELL, a shady showman
MONDAY
WEDNESDAY } his daughters
FRIDAY
FINNEY SLINE, a gold prospector
CORA, his daughter
LYDIA O. LYDIA, a woman of mystery
2 BUMPKINS

Place: The Cleanlivin Restaurant, somewhere in Old California.

Time: 1890

●

ACT I

Scene 1: Midmorning
Scene 2: The next day

ACT II: A few moments later

●

An earlier version of this play was given a staged reading at
Strand Street Theatre, Galveston, Texas, in 1985.

ABOUT THE PLAY

Here is another of Eddie Cope's light-hearted spoofs of nineteenth century American tragic drama which has been transformed through the decades and through incompetent management into comic melodrama. The playwright also takes a sidewinder swat at some of the treasured but well-worn cliches of today's serious, naturalistic drama, at Broadway musicals, and at show business in general.

Beneath the broad farce and slapstick, audiences at the staged reading in Galveston's Strand Street Theatre detected the author's subtle comments on some of the less attractive and little publicized mores of the intricate business known as theatre.

Ma and Pa Cleanlivin have an only son, Sonny. Instead of going into some honorable, useful business which could make his parents proud of him—such as football, wrestling, or streetcar conductoring—he goes off to the city to study (gasp, sputter, gag, choke) *dancing*. And then to add absurdity to ridiculousness, he tries to use his store-bought dance training to lift the old folks' run-down restaurant out of its bid for bankruptcy.

When it comes time to choose his chorus line, he meets that front line of defense that seems to protect so many theatre establishments from intrusion by talented newcomers: greed . . . personified by Col. Questus Quantrell. And a complete disregard for truth (are the triplets his daughters? Are the triplets triplets?).

Symbolism and satire aside, THE PERILOUS DECLINE OF CORA SLINE is designed for fun—the kind of fun that directors, cast members, and audiences alike find as refreshing as a cool drink after a heavy workout.

THE PERILOUS DECLINE OF CORA SLINE

or, Don't Touch My Tutu

ACT I

Scene 1

[Mid-morning in the sparse but neat Cleanlivin Restaurant (see Production Notes for floor plan). The place is empty except for PA CLEANLIVIN. Grizzled, aged, overweight, he stands Down Left, slamming his fist on the table. He wears a plaid shirt, dark pants, high-laced boots]

PA. Dad-blast it . . . dad-gum it . . . dad-dog it . . . *[He stops, grabs his chest, sinks weakly down into chair, groaning]* Hellllp . . .

MA. *[Enters from Right. She is middle-aged, wears a dowdy house-dress and apron]* Can't you see I'm busy in the kitchen.

PA. *[Gasping]* My ticker. I need one of my heart pills.

MA. We don't have any. Druggist cut off our credit because we're so far behind.

PA. That's where I'd like to kick him.

MA. Trouble with you is, you have Dunlap's Disease.

PA. Dunlap's Disease? What's that?

MA. Your stomach done laps over your belt.

PA. Never you mind. *[Working himself into a frenzy]* I'm sick, I tell you. Sick! *[He collapses against back of chair]* Anything could happen to me.

MA. Now don't go getting yourself worked up. I want you to be in a good mood, 'cause our boy's coming home this morning.

PA. 'Bout time he got a little sense.

MA. That'll be enough of that. He's leaving school to come help us out.

PA. Don't interrupt, Old Lady. It was your idea to send him to Frisco to study how to be a dancer. *[PA gets up to do a little dance step, but the effort is too much for him; he falls back into his chair]*

MA. Our Sonny's a good boy, and I'm proud of him . . .

PA. Hah! If he'd a-gone into something useful that would benefit mankind—like boxing or wrestling or football— *[Sound of galloping hooves; man off Left shouts: "Whoa!" Hoof-beats come to a screeching halt. MA leans toward Stage Left, hand to ear]*

MA. That's the stage coach . . . Sonny should be on it.

SONNY. *[Enters from Left. He's a handsome, lithe man, neatly dressed in a suit; he carries a large carpetbag]* Hello, everybody, I'm home.

MA. *[Hugs him]* My boy! *[PA makes a derisive but weak gesture]*

SONNY. I've missed you. *[He gets loose from her clutches, then shakes hands with his father]* Pa! Good to see you. *[PA pushes himself out of the chair]*

PA. This is a surprise. I half expected you to come through the door on tippy-toes. *[He awkwardly demonstrates; nearly falls over]*

SONNY. I came back to help out the family business . . . not to be made fun of.

MA. He's right, Pa. Get off his back.

PA. You make me tired, both of you. *[Falsetto]* "Get off'n his back."

MA. Sonny, you wrote that you had a great idea to perk up business. Want to tell us about it?

SONNY. Sure do. *[Takes a sign out of carpetbag, the lettered side of the sign turned away from the audience]*

PA. A blank sign! That's stupid.

MA. Pa!

PA. Even an old prospector like me knows you can't perk up business with a blank sign. *[To Sonny]* Get to the point or get out.

MA. Hush!

SONNY. You have to give the public a reason to patronize your establishment. Entertainment! I learned that from an advertising man in San Francisco.

PA. Listen, you young idiot, people come here to eat your Ma's good home cooking, not to see a dog and pony show.

SONNY. What people? *[Indicates the empty tables]*

PA. Wel-l-l-l . . . it's early . . . maybe later . . .

MA. Let's face it, Pa. Business is so bad even the cockroaches have deserted us.

SONNY. I'm trying to help, Pa. Please listen to me.

PA. Even if you had a good idea, it would be a bad idea.

MA. Shut up and listen at the boy.

PA. *[Grumbling]* Don't have nothing else to do. *[To Sonny]* Make it quick.

MA. Son, you take all the time you want. *[She makes a face at Pa]*

SONNY. I want to put in a dancing act. As the posters say—"ten beautiful girls, ten!" draped in flags of all nations! And right in the middle, posing like the Statue of Liberty, will be the most beautiful girl of all! *[He goes into a Statue of Liberty pose, holding the sign as though it were a torch]*

PA. Who, *you?* *[He laughs uproariously; SONNY is crestfallen]*

MA. *[Trying to suppress a laugh]* Pa, lay off the boy.

PA. *[Still laughing]* I can't help it. Besides, the doctor said that laughing is good for me. *[He does a poor imitation of Statue of Liberty]*

SONNY. Guess you don't think much of my idea.

MA. Never mind him. What is this sign you brought?

SONNY. *[Depressed]* What good would it do to show it?

MA. Now, Son.

SONNY. I don't want to waste anyone's time. Do you have any dirty dishes I can wash?

PA. The dog done beat you to it.

SONNY. Huh?

PA. *[Picks up dish from table and licks it]* And even the dog is starving. *[Bursts out laughing]*

MA. Never mind that old fool. We want to see the sign.

SONNY. I'm sorry I brought it. *[Holds up sign, which reads "Dancers Wanted. Apply Within." MA takes the sign]*

MA. Let me put it in the front window.

PA. *[Grabbing sign]* Oh, no you don't. *[They have a tug-of-war with the sign during the following lines]*

MA. Oh, yes I do.

PA. I won't let you.

MA. Oh, yes you will.

PA. Over my dead . . . *[He breaks off the tug-of-war; coughs violently; holds his heart. SONNY crosses to him, concerned]*

SONNY. What's the matter?

MA. *[Wrenching the sign out of his hand]* Sit down, Pa, and catch your breath while you still have some to catch. *[To Sonny]* He'll be all right.

SONNY. Pa, let me help you. *[MA tiptoes out door Left, taking sign with her. SONNY holds his father up]* Pa, you don't look well. Maybe you'd better lie down in your room.

PA. *[Weakly]* Thank you, Son. *[He leans on SONNY as they cross to door Up Right]* I'm mighty sorry if I talked mean to you.

SONNY. That's all right. *[He props Pa against door, goes back to *pick up his carpetbag; then SONNY walks his father out. As they exit we hear PA say:]*

PA. But *dancin'*! Why can't you take up a trade that'll last forever— like streetcar conductorin'.

[After a beat, two young country BUMPKINS, dressed in overalls, cautiously enter from Left. They look around the room, chuckle oafishly; then they push and punch one another. More chuckling. SONNY enters Up Right]

SONNY. Ah, good morning, gentlemen! Are you here to audition? *[The two BUMPKINS guffaw nervously, nudge one another]* Step up on the platform. *[Guffawing, the two BUMPKINS dash out door Left; MA is entering and is spun around, then takes a pratfall]* Mother, are you all right?

MA. *[Picking herself up]* I . . . I guess so . . .

SONNY. H'm. They came in to audition, but changed their minds.

MA. Oh, you wouldn't want them anyway. Just a coupla country clods. All they do is hang out at the Sheriff's office.

SONNY. *[Shrugs]* Ma . . . I'm worried about Pa.

MA. It's his own fault. Every time he gets excited, he has one of those heart spasms.

SONNY. What does the doctor say?

MA. We can't afford to go to him any more.

SONNY. Speaking of heart spasms, Ma, there's something I have to tell you.

MA. What is it, Son?

SONNY. *[Uncomfortable]* I think I'm in love.

MA. That's nice.

SONNY. I'm serious.

MA. Of course you are, dear. How does she feel about you?

SONNY. I don't know.

MA. Where's she from?

SONNY. I don't know.

MA. What's her name?

SONNY. I don't know.

MA. *[Angrily]* Quit saying "I don't know" until you know something.

SONNY. I know this much: She got on the stagecoach when we stopped at Sutter's Mill.

MA. Sutter's Mill? That's gold-mining country.

COLONEL. *[Off Left]* This is the place, girls.
GIRLS. *[Off Left, giggling]* Ooooooh.

*[COLONEL enters with audition sign. COLONEL QUESTUS QUAN-
TRELL is a typical villain: tall, dark, and snarling; wearing tophat,
black cape, black suit, black gloves. He is a tentshow impresario who
is temporarily "at liberty." His only clients are the no-talent QUAN-
TRELL TRIPLETS, who follow him in]*

COLONEL. Ring the bell, here's Quantrell . . . with the world-famous
Quantrell Triplets!
GIRLS. *[Speaking simultaneously]* Hello, folks.
   Hi, everybody.
   Howdy, howdy, howdy.
COLONEL. *[Holding up sign]* Who gets this?
MA. My son is in charge of entertainment.
COLONEL. *[Handing sign to Sonny]* Here you go, kid. Now shake
hands with Colonel Questus Quantrell, impresario, showman de luxe,
actor, director, producer, playwright, hypnotist, prestidigitator, owner,
operator, proprietor, booking agent, and man about women.
   GIRLS. *[They are mismatched young women, each dressed in an ug-
ly long black dress. All wear too much make-up, crudely applied. Each
carries a small handbag or straw suitcase. They applaud the Colonel after
he finishes his opening speech]* Bravo!
   SONNY. I'm sorry, sir, but I am looking for dancers . . . not actresses
for the opening scene of "Macbeth."
   MA. *[To audience]* He means the witches.
   COLONEL. My girls are the finest dancers in all Californy. Permit
me to introduce them. Mr. . . . . uh?
   SONNY. *[Shaking hands]* Sonny Cleanlivin. And this is my mother,
Mrs. Cleanlivin.
   COLONEL. The pressure is mine. *[He steps close to Ma and swings
watch fob in front of her face, as he stares at her]*
   MA. *[Recoiling]* Are you trying to cast a spell over me?
   COLONEL. *[Bows]* And now you must meet my triplets. *[As he
calls each name, a different girl curtsies]* Monday . . . Wednesday . . . Fri-
day.
   MA. May I ask why you named them after days of the week?
   COLONEL. You may.
   MA. Why did you name them after days of the week?

COLONEL. Because each was born on that particular day.

MA. *[To audience]* Triplets? Monday through Friday? I hope their mother got overtime pay for all that labor.

COLONEL. *[To Ma]* And, now, let us leave the young people alone so that your son can get on with the audition.

MA. Perhaps you will step into my kitchen and join me in a bowl of soup.

COLONEL. I'd be glad to, providing you have a large enough bowl. *[They exit Right. SONNY stares at the girls with annoyance]*

GIRLS. *[Speaking simultaneously]* Well, let's go.

I'm ready if you are.

What're we waiting for?

Let's get started.

Wanna see my cancan?

SONNY. Hold it, hold it! *[GIRLS continue chattering; SONNY shouts:]* Quiet! All of you! *[GIRLS shut up]* Firstly, there's not going to be an audition. You girls are not what I'm looking for. So don't call me and I won't call you. *[He begins to exit. GIRLS crowd around him]*

MONDAY. What if we insist?

SONNY. It would be a waste of time.

WEDNESDAY. Mister, we don't like your addletude.

SONNY. Sorry about that. *[Tries to leave]*

MONDAY. Sisters, shall we *demand* a audition?

GIRLS. We demand a audition! *[They produce pistols and point them at Sonny]*

SONNY. *[Stunned]* Hey . . . wha—?

FRIDAY. How soon do we start?

SONNY. Immediately. *[All businesslike]* Girls, get up on the stage, then form a straight line. *[GIRLS put pistols in their pockets, step up on platform, form a line facing the Up Center wall]* No, no, no! You're facing the wrong way! *[GIRLS turn around in all directions; now, one is facing Left, one is facing Right, one is facing front]* Girls, the audience is this way. Face me. *[They do so]* Now I want to see a simple softshoe time step. Five, six, seven, eight. *[He sings]* "Way down upon the Swanee River, la, la, la" . . . No, no, no! You're supposed to be dancing, not stomping grapes!

WEDNESDAY. This dance is too hard.

FRIDAY. Give us more time.

SONNY. We'll get back to dancing later. But first, I want each of you to step front and center . . . and— *[All three start crowding into the center spot]* No, no, no! One at a time. *[They back off]* Who's first? You.

FRIDAY. My name's Friday. I'm the oldest.

SONNY. *[To audience]* Something's wrong here. *[To Friday]* Tell me about yourself.

FRIDAY. I am a very good dancer. *[SONNY looks at audience and rolls his eyes heavenward]* And my hobby is collecting handguns.

SONNY. Next!

WEDNESDAY. At an early age, my daddy taught me how to use a pistol. Oh, yes, my name is Wednesday and I just love to dance.

SONNY. Now, you.

MONDAY. My name is Monday.

SONNY. Go on.

MONDAY. I worked in Buffalo Bill's Wild West Show.

SONNY. What did you do?

MONDAY. I did an Indian dance. Then I shot a feather offa Annie Oakley's head.

SONNY. Uh-huh.

MONDAY. Annie Oakley and me worked as a team.

SONNY. *[To audience]* Pulling a wagon, no doubt.

GIRLS. When do we eat?

SONNY. OK. Take ten.

MONDAY. Ten plates of food?

SONNY. *[Groans and holds his head in despair, points Right]* The kitchen's in there . . . and I'm going to take a nap. *[Giggling, the GIRLS hurry out Right; SONNY exits Up Right]*

[The stage is empty for a moment, then a grizzled, aged prospector, leaning on a beautiful young lady, enters from Left. FINNEY SLINE and his daughter CORA each carry a small handbag. CORA wears a pink tutu and ballet slippers; FINNEY is dressed like a prospector. She dusts off her father's shoulders and a large cloud of dust fills the air]

FINNEY. Thank you, my love. *[Fans the dust away with his hands]*

CORA. I am doing what any dutiful daughter would do. *[She continues to dust off his shoulders]*

FINNEY. Just don't overdo.

CORA. Father, dear father, why did you ask me to bring you to this empty, run-down restaurant?

FINNEY. Don't know how to break the news, gal.

CORA. Please try.

FINNEY. We've never been very close. There I was in the Californy back country prospecting for gold, while you was gettin' raised up and educated in Boston.

CORA. Why are you telling me all this?

FINNEY. For the audience's benefit. *[To audience]* It's called exposition!

CORA. You are quite right. We've never been very close till I decided to look you up . . . after all these years.

FINNEY. I hate to tell you this, gal, but . . . I'm dying.

CORA. Oh, how you do go on.

FINNEY. Since I'm not long for this world, I wanted to look up my old partner and heal some deep wounds.

CORA. Oh, Father, are you wounded?

FINNEY. Hear me out. Dirty Cleanlivin and I were gold prospectors many years ago. We had a bitter falling out over a lady. We both loved her, but she consented to give me her hand in marriage. Then you came along and she carried you away to Boston. And I never saw either of you again until last month when you came to Sutter's Mill.

CORA. Yes, Father.

FINNEY. I want to settle up with Dirty Cleanlivin. Most of all, I want to give him this confidential letter. *[Takes letter out of coat pocket]* Personally.

CORA. What is the letter about?

FINNEY. Didn't you hear me say it was confidential?!

CORA. Oh.

FINNEY. Don't interrupt any more. I'm sinking fast. *[Gasps for breath]* About that letter . . . I cannot disclose the contents to anyone except my ex-partner. He's the only one I can trust to see that you git what what's comin' to you. *[Gasps]* Hurry and find Dirty Cleanlivin.

CORA. Better yet, I'll hunt up a doctor. *[She seats him at Down Right table and pirouettes out Left]*

FINNEY. *[Groaning]* Ohhhhhh . . .

PA. *[Steps into room from Up Right, cups his ear and leans sideways]* Did I hear someone groaning?

FINNEY. *[Facing front; weakly]* I'm in heaven and I hear the voice of my old partner.

PA. Did I hear the voice of . . .? *[Looks Right, looks Left, finally *looks right in front of him and sees Finney seated at the table]* Do my eyes deceive me? Are you Finney—Finney Sline! *[He rushes to FIN-NEY, who weakly gets to his feet]*

FINNEY. Yes. Are you Dirty?

PA. Usually. *[They embrace and pat each other's shoulder blades weakly]* I've missed you, old pardner.

FINNEY. Same here. *[Weakly waves envelope]*

PA. Why are you fanning me with that envelope? You'll wear yourself out.

FINNEY. It don't matter. I've washed my last pan of gold.

PA. What is this envelope you keep flashing?

FINNEY. It's a deep, dark secret.

PA. Who knows about it except you?

FINNEY. No one. That's why it's a deep, dark secret. *[Gasps]* When I die, which will be soon, I want you to tell this information to my darling daughter Cora.

PA. If that's all you want, why be so mysterious?

FINNEY. Because there's something else in this envelope.

PA. Are you going to tell me or ain't you?

FINNEY. Don't get obstreperous with me.

PA. Who's getting ob— whatever you said.

FINNEY. You are.

PA. I ain't either.

FINNEY. If I say you are, then you are!

PA. You haven't changed, have you!

FINNEY. What do you mean by that?

PA. Always trying to shove me around. *[Shoves Finney weakly—but it staggers FINNEY]*

FINNEY. Don't you push me!

PA. I will if I want to.

FINNEY. Then take that! *[He swings at Pa, but misses and nearly falls. FINNEY gasps and grabs his heart]*

PA. And you take this! *[He swings at Finney but misses and nearly falls. PA coughs and grabs his heart. They both pant and wheeze]*

FINNEY. Dirty! I'm dead!

PA. Finney! I'm finished! *[Weakly]* Please . . . please . . . tell me your deep, dark secret . . . before I shuffle off this morbid soil . . .

FINNEY. Parting is such lousy sorrow. *[Holds up envelope; says weakly]* This envelope . . . contains . . . contains . . . *[He gasps, rattles, and dies. The envelope falls to the floor. PA reaches for the envelope—gasps, rattles, and dies. MA enters from Right, stops behind Pa, looks down at him, then runs to Up Right door screaming]*

MA. Sonny!

PA. *[Gets up on one elbow and says to audience:]* Just kidding, folks. Wanted to see how my Old Lady would react. Hee, hee—she's heart-broken. *[MA's screams turn out to be hilarious laughter. She kicks her heels and lets out a loud joyful whoop]*

MA. At last, I'm free. I'm free! It took the old mule long enough to ride to his last roundup. *[She happily dances out Right. PA's face falls; then PA falls . . . really dead this time. A moment later, CORA runs in from door Left]*

CORA. The doctor was out of town and . . . Father! What's the matter? *[She hurries to him and feels his pulse, then shakes her head sadly]* He's gone to that great gold gulch in the sky! And what of this other gentleman? *[She feels Pa's pulse]* Alas, he, too, is gone. Two dead men are almost too much for me. I am faint. *[She picks up the envelope and fans herself]* Oh, woe is me . . . a young girl, alone and penniless in the world . . . *[She takes a tablecloth off one of the tables and covers the men; then she puts envelope on the table and cries loudly. COLONEL sticks his head out of door Right and cups his ear]*

COLONEL. Do I hear the sound of a damsel in disarray?

CORA. *[Stops crying to say:]* "Distress." *[Resumes crying]*

COLONEL. *[To audience]* Ah, a true beauty . . . pure as the driven sky.

CORA. *[Stops crying to say:]* "Snow." *[Resumes crying]*

COLONEL. Young lady, I am trying to help you, so please don't put cliches in my mouth.

CORA. I beg your pardon, sir. *[Wipes tears from her eyes]*

COLONEL. That's more like it.

CORA. Great sorrow has just enveloped me. My father is no more.

COLONEL. *[Sees envelope on table]* Speaking of envelopes, allow me to fan you. *[He picks up envelope and fans her]* This benighted hash-house is hot as a fireplace.

CORA. "Firecracker."

COLONEL. *[Angrily]* Stop that! *[He puts envelope on table and becomes very solicitous]* Forgive me, my sweet, I did not mean to speak harshly. *[Elaborate bow]* Permit me to introduce myself. I am Colonel Questus Quantrell, self-made impresario extraordinary.

CORA. Pleased to meet you, sir. My name is Cora Sline.

COLONEL. *[Another elaborate bow]* The pressure is all mine, Miss Sline.

CORA. I am a graduate of BATS.

COLONEL. Bats? You mean ... *[He flaps his arms and makes squeaking sounds]*

CORA. No, sir. B-A-T-S. Boston Academy of Terpsichore and Speech.

COLONEL. How impressive! And what are you going to do now that your father has gone to his reveille?

CORA. "Reward." I do not know, sir. I am alone in the world and penniless.

COLONEL. How sad!

CORA. There's nothing to support me but my two lower limbs.

COLONEL. *[To audience]* That's the way I like to hear a girl talk. *[To Cora]* Then you must allow me to befriend you.

CORA. But, sir, it would not be proper to depend on the kindness of strangers. *[She buries her head in her arms and cries]*

COLONEL. You sound exactly like a girl named Blanche DeBow I used to know. *[Laughs coarsely and loudly. SONNY sticks his head out of door Up Right and cups his ear. He reacts when he recognizes Cora. He tiptoes to door Right, opens it, then whispers:]*

SONNY. Mother!

MA. *[Stands in doorway]* Yes?

SONNY. There she is!

MA. There *who* is?

SONNY. *[Pointing to Cora; still crying, she does not see Sonny. But the COLONEL listens with a dramatic pose]* The girl on the stagecoach ... the girl I am in love with ... the girl I am going to marry!

COLONEL. *[Aside]* Heh-heh-heh. He won't want her after I get through with the little wench. *[Rubs his hands together and continues his coarse laughter]*

CURTAIN

Scene 2

[The next morning. SONNY is trying to teach the QUANTRELL girls a simple dance routine. They are hopeless. They are wearing 1890's rehearsal clothes: bloomers, middy tops, old-fashioned bathing suits, high-button shoes, hair ribbons, etc. Each girl is dressed differently and, of course, sloppily. It is obvious that SONNY is beginning to run out of patience]

SONNY. Let's try it again. Five, six, seven, eight. *[Sings]* "Way down upon the Swanee River, far . . ." *[The GIRLS run into each other]* Hold it! Hold it! *[Two of the GIRLS stop dancing, but MONDAY, whose head is in the clouds, continues an ungainly solo]* Everybody hold it! *[MONDAY continues dancing]* What's your name?
MONDAY. *[Still dancing]* Monday.
SONNY. Didn't you hear me tell you to stop?
MONDAY. *[Still dancing]* I just feel like dancing.
SONNY. *[Angrily]* I'm in charge here. And when I give you an order to stop, you stop.
MONDAY. *[Still dancing, she takes a pistol out of her pocket and points it at Sonny]* Will you please repeat that.
SONNY. I forgot what I said. *[He sits at table, picks up the envelope and fans himself with it]*
MONDAY. *[Finally stops dancing]* I'm pooped. *[Fans herself with her hand]* I'm also hungry.
GIRLS. Me, too.
     Let's eat.
     Food, food. *[GIRLS run out door Right. SONNY steps up on platform and works on a simple softshoe step. Stops and muses like a lovesick schoolboy]*
SONNY. Oh, Cora, Cora, you are the girl of my dreams. *[Pause]* H'm, that gives me an idea for a song. *[Sings a few bars:]* "Girl of my dreams, I love you . . ." *[He resumes dancing as CORA and MA, dressed in black mourning clothes (Cora's mourning costume is a black tutu), enter from Left. They stand inside door for a moment to watch Sonny. They applaud]*
MA. Don't let us interrupt you, son.
SONNY. I was just working up an idea.
CORA. May I work with you?
SONNY. That would be an honor and an inspiration.

MA. *[Sniffs the air]* Something's burning in my kitchen. Who could be in there?

SONNY. The triplets are having their second breakfast.

MA. I'm going in there and give those girls a mouth full! *[Exits Right]*

SONNY. At last we are together.

CORA. "Alone." *[They embrace passionately]* I keep thinking how you proposed to me last night on the back porch of the funeral parlor.

SONNY. We had to do something to take our minds off the tragedy of our fathers.

CORA. I didn't see you at the services this morning.

SONNY. There was this dance rehearsal with the triplets.

CORA. *[Slightly critical]* Well, you could have canceled the rehearsal. It wasn't as though someone held a gun on you.

SONNY. *[To audience]* If she only knew.

CORA. Where's that nice Colonel Quantrell?

SONNY. He's a late sleeper. *[Indicates door Up Right]* Never mind him, let's talk about us.

CORA. When should we set our wedding date?

SONNY. The sooner, the better. But it won't be a stylish marriage, because we can't affort a buggy. *[Crosses to table]*

CORA. "Carriage."

SONNY. *[Idly fans himself with the envelope]* Oh, if we could only get our hands on some money.

CORA. That would be a miracle, and miracles only happen in books.

SONNY. We'll make our own miracles. Kiss me, my love.

CORA. My Boston headmistress wouldn't like it.

SONNY. No, but I would. *[They kiss demurely. COLONEL enters, yawning, from Up Right]*

COLONEL. Why didn't someone wake me? *[Sees young couple embracing. He strides over to them and roughly tears them apart]* Miss Sline, is this young scoundrel forcing his attentions on you?

SONNY. I'll answer that.

COLONEL. I want to hear it from her lips.

CORA. Sir . . .

SONNY. We don't owe him any explanation.

COLONEL. I demand an explanation.

CORA. *[To Sonny]* Let me handle this.

COLONEL. Better yet, let my friend Colt handle the situation. *[Pulls gun on Sonny]* Keep out of this.

CORA. Please do what the man says.

SONNY. Will you think any the less of my manhood?

CORA. Of course not.

SONNY. *[Sings as he does a traveling step]* "Way down upon the Swanee . . ." *[Exits Left. CORA is disappointed]*

CORA. I thought he was more of a man than that.

COLONEL. Why do you waste your time with a bum like him?

CORA. Other than you, he is the only one who has befriended me in this town.

COLONEL. My dear, you are like a daughter to me.

CORA. And you are like a father to me.

COLONEL. Daughter! *[He hugs her. She struggles out of his embrace]*

CORA. Please don't be so fatherly.

COLONEL. Excuse me. I was carried away. I do the same thing with my offspring.

CORA. Oh, then you are a family man.

COLONEL. Unfortunately, my sweet wife passed away, so I raised the girls myself and put them into show business.

CORA. What kind of act do they have?

COLONEL. They're dancers. They float around a stage like angels.

CORA. What a coincidence. I, too, float around a stage like an angel.

COLONEL. Forsooth.

CORA. For truth.

COLONEL. Could you do a few steps for me?

CORA. I cannot work without a dance director.

COLONEL. No problem. Let me instruct you.

CORA. Splendid idea. *[She goes into a graceful pose, indicating that she is ready to begin dancing]*

COLONEL. Oh, not here, child.

CORA. Where then?

COLONEL. In my private rehearsal hall. *[Indicates door Up Right]* I'll teach you some new positions—for the ballet.

CORA. But that's where your bedroom is.

COLONEL. *[To audience]* This kid is no dummy. *[To Cora]* You must not mistake my motives, girl.

CORA. I must be careful. As I told you . . . or somebody . . . I am all alone in this world . . . and penniless.

COLONEL. Would you mistrust a father?

CORA. A real father or a . . .

COLONEL. . . . or a famous producer who has the power to put your name in candles?

CORA. H'mmmmm. *[Pause]* Let me think about it.

COLONEL. There's no time to waste. I want you now . . . for a dancing lesson. *[Stares at her, hypnotically, swings watch fob]*

CORA. No.

COLONEL. *[He grabs her]* I will not take "no" for a response.

CORA. "Answer." *[Pause]* And don't try to mesmerize me.

COLONEL. You'll rue the day you spurned my advances. *[Starts chasing her around the tables]*

SONNY. *[Enters from Left; stands inside door and goes into a heroic pose]* Muscles to the rescue. *[He leaps on the COLONEL, who pulls a gun. SONNY wrests the gun away and holds it on the villain, who has fallen to the floor]* On your feet, lecherous scum!

CORA. My hero! You have saved me from a death worse than fate. *[She hugs Sonny]*

VOICE IN AUDIENCE. Fate worse than death! *[Meanwhile, COLONEL has been getting to his feet slowly]*

COLONEL. For your information, the gun isn't loaded.

SONNY. Then I shall pull the trigger and verify your statement.

COLONEL. *[Terrified]* No, please! Don't shoot me! Don't shoot me.

SONNY. Sir, you are a rotter, through and through.

CORA. He tried to hypnotize me into going to his private studio to show me some new positions.

SONNY. But he is not a dance director.

COLONEL. How dare you contradict me?

SONNY. Then let me see you do a simple time step.

COLONEL. I don't have the time.

SONNY. Do you want me to click this "unloaded" gun at your feet?

COLONEL. No, no, please! *[He looks over his shoulder at door Up Right]* But you must let me don my dancing slippers.

SONNY. Where are they?

COLONEL. In my bedroo— I mean, in my private dance studio.

SONNY. Go get them.

COLONEL. Yes, sir. *[He exits Up Right]*

CORA. Oh, Sonny boy, you are so masterful. I'm sorry I ever doubted your manhood. *[She hugs him]* We must never be parted again.

SONNY. Never a truer word was uttered.

CORA. "Spoken."

COLONEL. *[Sticks his head out door Up Right]* Anyone have a shoehorn?

SONNY. Use a tablespoon.

COLONEL. Thanks. *[Exits Up Right]*

SONNY. Where were we?

CORA. I said, "We must never be parted . . ."

SONNY. Then I said, "Use a tablespoon."

MA. *[Sticks her head out door Right]* Cora, could I see you for a moment?

CORA. Yes, ma'am. *[To Sonny]* Please excuse me. *[She runs out door Right]*

SONNY. *[Shouting after her]* While you're out, I'll try to remember where we were.

[LYDIA O. LYDIA, a middle-aged, overdressed, over-painted woman, enters from Left. She wears a hat, scarf, gloves, low-cut dress; stands in doorway as she looks fearfully at the sky and says to herself:]

LYDIA. The sun looks so strange. Something tragic is about to happen. *[Aloud]* Hey, you!

SONNY. Are you speaking to me?

LYDIA. You're the only one in the lobby, aren't you?

SONNY. Lady, if you're looking for a hotel . . .?

LYDIA. *[Interrupting]* I know what I'm looking for.

SONNY. This is the Cleanlivin Restaurant.

LYDIA. Right!

SONNY. Then, may I show you to a table?

LYDIA. Later. Meantime, they told me at the stagecoach office I'd find a certain gentleman here.

SONNY. Oh, I'm sorry.

LYDIA. What the heck are you sorry about?

SONNY. The gentleman you are in search of . . .

LYDIA. Yeah?

SONNY. . . . died yesterday.

LYDIA. *[Stunned]* No!

SONNY. Sorry to say . . . yes.

LYDIA. My heart is broken.

SONNY. So is mine.

LYDIA. *[Hugging him]* We must console each other.

CORA. *[Enters from Right]* Sonny, I just rememb— *[She sees Son-*

ny and Lydia in an embrace] Oh, the fickleness of muscular men. *[SON-
NY struggles to get out of Lydia's grasp, but can't. CORA hurries to
door Up Right]* Colonel Quantrell, I'm ready for that dance lesson. Can
you accommodate me immediately? *[A hand reaches out and pulls her
off Up Right. SONNY finally extricates himself, shouts to Cora]*

SONNY. Cora! No, you mustn't!
LYDIA. What the heck are you talking about?
SONNY. My girl. I must rescue her.
LYDIA. From what?
SONNY. Disgrace and degradation. *[He goes into his heroic pose]*
LYDIA. Young man, don't get so melodramatic. Maybe I can help
you.
SONNY. He's a scoundrel of the worst degree. Takes a young girl to
his private dance studio and promises to put her name in candles.
LYDIA. Candles? Saaay . . . are we thinking about the same scoun-
drel?
SONNY. Colonel Quantrell.
LYDIA. But you said he died yesterday.
SONNY. My *father* died yesterday.
LYDIA. Where is the Colonel's studio?
SONNY. He doesn't have one.
LYDIA. Where does he hang his pants?
SONNY. In there. *[Points Up Right]*
LYDIA. Drag him out.
SONNY. *[Pounds on door]* Colonel, there's a lady here to see you.
COLONEL. *[Off]* What's her name?
SONNY. *[To Lydia]* What's your name?
LYDIA. Lydia O. Lydia.
SONNY. Lydia O. Lydia?
LYDIA. Yes.
SONNY. *[Facing door]* Lydia O. Lydia.
COLONEL. *[Off]* Ask her if she has a shoehorn.
LYDIA. I'll shoehorn him. *[Dashes through door Up Right. MA en-
ters Right]*
MA. Sonny, what's all the noise out here?
SONNY. Things are happening.
MA. I've got to talk to you.
SONNY. Can we please make it some other time?
MA. It won't wait. It's about those scalawagging Quantrell females.

SONNY. Oh . . .?

MA. They're eating me out of kitchen and restaurant.

SONNY. Why do you bother with them?

MA. They're armed and dangerous, that's why.

SONNY. *[Goes into a thinking pose]* There must be a way of getting those guns away from them. I'll think of a plan.

MA. Oh, Son, I'm so discouraged. *[Sits and fans herself with the envelope]* Spent our last penny on the funeral . . . now we're going to lose the restaurant. If we just knew where to find some money . . .

SONNY. *[Heroic pose]* We mustn't give up.

MA. That's easy for you to declaim.

SONNY. *[Patting her on the back]* Be of good cheer, dear. *[Pause]* Hear?

MA. Good cheer, my rear! *[SONNY looks at her in surprise]* I mean, my foot! Which reminds me, my right shoe is plumb wore out. *[Removes shoe]*

SONNY. You poor soul.

MA. This envelope has been laying around on the table since yesterday; now it'll come in handy. *[Puts envelope in shoe. Stands up]* My, that feels better.

SONNY. Ma, I want to talk to you.

MA. Of course, son.

SONNY. You know that girl I told you about?

MA. Yes. Cora Sline. A splendid little person.

SONNY. That splendid little person jilted me. She prefers Quantrell. *[He sits, then buries his face in his crossed arms on table. GIRLS enter from Right. One has napkin tied around her neck, another is picking her teeth, another is wiping her mouth on her sleeve]*

MONDAY. I just saw a Western roach.

MA. How do you know it's a Western roach?

GIRLS. Because it's on the range.

WEDNESDAY. *[Noticing Sonny]* What's the matter with Prettyboy?

MA. He's thinking up a new routine. Don't disturb him.

GIRLS. *[All put index fingers to their lips]* Sssssssh.

SONNY. *[Getting up slowly]* Ah!

MA. He's getting it.

SONNY. Yes, indeed. *[Dramatic stance; hand on forehead]* I have— I have an idea . . .

GIRLS. We're ready.

Lay it on us.

Tell us about it.

Let's have it.

SONNY. First of all, this routine will require that you not be weighted down with any heavy encumbrances. *[He pauses to let that sink in]* So if you have any weighty metal objects . . . such as firearms . . . please give them to my mother for safekeeping.

GIRLS. Now?

SONNY. Right now. *[GIRLS put guns on table]* Everybody on stage! *[MA absently follows GIRLS toward stage]* NOT YOU, MOTHER!!

MA. Oh . . .

SONNY. *[Talking to her as if she were a child]* Gather up the guns and take them to the kitchen for safekeeping. *[He points Right]* There.

MA. *[Mumbling to herself]* Gather up the guns . . . *[She does so, then starts for door Right. At that moment COLONEL enters from Up Right]*

COLONEL. I need a tablesp— *[He sees MA leaving with her hands full of guns. Angrily:]* What are you doing with those pistols?

MA. Taking them to the kitchen for safekeeping.

COLONEL. You'll do nothing of the sort.

MA. But Sonny said . . .

COLONEL. *[Interrupting]* I don't care what anyone said. Those guns are never to leave the person of my girls. Is that understood? *[Swings watch fob in front of her]*

MA. Yes, sir.

COLONEL. Return them to their rightful owners.

MA. Yes, sir. *[She crosses hypnotically to the Girls. COLONEL follows]*

SONNY. I have something to say about that.

COLONEL. I'm not interested in anything you have to say, punk. *[He leans threateningly toward Sonny]*

MA. Don't argue with the man. He's got us out-gunned.

SONNY. *[As COLONEL angrily takes guns from Ma and passes them to his daughters]* There's a kernel of truth in what you say.

GIRLS. Let's eat.

I'm hungry.

So am I.

We'll rehearse later.

MA. *[Annoyed]* You know where the kitchen is. *[She stomps out Right, followed by GIRLS. CORA and LYDIA enter from Up Right.*

LYDIA is demonstrating some hand gestures to Cora, who is repeating them. It is all very amiable]

CORA. Thanks for teaching me those dance gestures.

LYDIA. You catch on very fast. Keep practicing. *[CORA stands in Up Right area practicing, while LYDIA crosses to Colonel and then walks him away from Sonny]* How's the food in this joint?

COLONEL. Terrible.

LYDIA. Then let's go someplace else.

COLONEL. Not on your life.

LYDIA. Why not?

COLONEL. This food is free. I've got the old lady under my spell.

LYDIA. Let's eat then.

COLONEL. You go ahead. I have to get something from my room. *[He exits Up Right]*

LYDIA. Don't be too long. *[She exits Right]*

CORA. Sonny . . .

SONNY. *[Hurries to her]* At last we are by ourselves! *[He starts to embrace her, but she pushes him away]*

CORA. I want to talk to you.

SONNY. We can always talk. Let's fling ourselves into each other's arms first.

CORA. We'll do nothing of the sort.

SONNY. I . . . I don't understand.

CORA. I do not approve of the way you conduct yourself. The Colonel convinced me that I should sever connections with you. He said you have no gumption.

SONNY. What else did the great Colonel say?

CORA. He convinced me that I should be the lead dancer in his troupe. We'll travel.

SONNY. What does Miss Lydia say about that?

CORA. *She* wants to be the lead dancer.

SONNY. Ah-ha, the plot is beginning to get sticky.

CORA. The Colonel solved everything.

SONNY. I'll bet.

CORA. He's going to start up a new troupe that will open on Broadway, and Miss Lydia will be the star of that company.

SONNY. What a neat arrangement.

CORA. Yes, indeed. The Colonel will spend one week with our troupe, then he'll spend the next week with the Broadway company. Back and forth, back and forth.

SONNY. I hope the Pony Express travels that fast.

CORA. So, if you'll pardon me, I want to do a few warmup steps. *[She goes to platform and starts to warm up]*

SONNY. *[Crossing to her]* Please, Cora, I cannot bear to have you dance except under my auspices.

CORA. Away with you. I'm too busy to talk.

SONNY. Agony, agony. Oh, ag-gone-neee!

CORA. Will you leave or will I have to call the Colonel?

SONNY. I go, but with a heart that is wrenched.

CORA. "Broken."

SONNY. Both. *[He tragically sings "Way down upon the Swanee River" and does a mournful travel step all the way to his exit Left. CORA resumes her warmup activities; suddenly all the LIGHTS go out. In the total darkness a gun is fired offstage. Slowly the LIGHTS come up. CORA is lying dead on the edge of the platform. All at once, the stage is full of people. Near the kitchen door: MA, LYDIA, and GIRLS. At door Up Right: COLONEL. At door Left: SONNY. Note: if the director desires, several Towspeople can be standing with Sonny. Everyone is aghast. SONNY runs over to Cora and feels her pulse. He tragically rises to his full height and looks skyward]* Alas, this beautiful child will dance no more. Someone killed her during the total eclipse.

CURTAIN

ACT II

[A few moments later. All are in same positions as before. SONNY takes a cloth off table Up Left and covers Cora, pausing only to lower his face close to hers for a moment]

SONNY. Good night, sweet princess. *[Sadly crosses to table Down Left]* And flights of angels sing thee to thy rest. *[SONNY sits. ALL applaud]*

ALL. You got it.

Well said.

Gee, you're smart.

Knows his Shakespeare.

Bravo.

SONNY. *[Sadly takes a bow]* Thank you, thank you. *[Sits and buries his face in his hands. MA crosses and sits beside him]*

MA. My poor boy. *[Hugs him. COLONEL crosses to a point near table Down Right; LYDIA joins him]*

COLONEL. What a waste.

LYDIA. What do you mean by that?

COLONEL. *[Pats his stomach]* She had a very trim waist.

LYDIA. I'm not much larger through the middle . . . and you've never bragged about me.

COLONEL. Ah, but you have great maturity, my dear.

LYDIA. Are you calling me an old hag?

COLONEL. Quite the contrary. *[To audience]* I'm calling her an old bag. *[They sit at table Down Right and converse silently]*

MA. First your father, now your intended.

SONNY. You and I, we're the last of the Cleanlivin line.

MA. All alone and broke.

SONNY. Now that Cora's gone, I'll never leave you. *[He lowers his head onto his crossed arms; MA rubs his back]*

LYDIA. Questus, circumstances have played into our hands.

COLONEL. Meaning?

LYDIA. You now need a lead dancer for the touring company.

COLONEL. By jove, you're right.

LYDIA. You've got me. We'll be able to travel together permanently.

COLONEL. I've got to think this over.

LYDIA. *[Angrily]* Are you casting me aside like an old slipper?

COLONEL. Of course not, my dear, only . . .

LYDIA. Only what?

COLONEL. *[Stands up and dramatizes]* Only I think of you as a great soloist . . . a star performer . . . someone who deserves to be on stage alone.

LYDIA. *[Slowly, dramatically, she gets to her feet and preens]* The stardom I so richly deserve . . . all by myself in the spotlight . . . adored by the entire populace . . .

COLONEL. Yes, indeed.

LYDIA. *[Realistically]* H'mmmm. I'll need a designer . . . a writer . . . a musical director . . . an electrician . . . and most important of all . . . a dance director.

COLONEL. *[To audience]* As the monkey said when he cried into the cash register, "This is going to run into money." *[They sit at table Down Right and silently talk conspiratorially]*

MA. Feeling better, son?

SONNY. Little bit.

MA. Anything I can do for you?

SONNY. Keep rubbing my back.

MA. Here?

SONNY. A little lower. *[GIRLS, all the while, have been standing in front of door Right. MONDAY takes the iniative and crosses to table Up Right. The others follow. They all sit as they speak]*

MONDAY. My dogs are barking.

WEDNESDAY. I'm pooped.

FRIDAY. Me, too.

LYDIA. *[To Colonel]* If we could just get our hands on some quick cash. *[Thinks for a moment]* I've got it! We'll hire a dance director we don't have to pay.

COLONEL. Who'd be stupid enough to work for nothing? *[Thinks a moment, turns to audience]* All of us actors in this play.

LYDIA. The kid.

COLONEL. *[Indicating Sonny]* You mean . . . *him?*

LYDIA. Why not?

COLONEL. What does he know . . . except Frisco-style dancing.

LYDIA. *[In a Mae West tone]* What he don't know, I can teach him.

COLONEL. Do you think we can pry him loose from his mama? Look at him. She's rubbing his back and he's coming unglued.

LYDIA. I'll remind him what happened to his sweetheart.

COLONEL. *[Using his hand like a pistol]* Bang, bang, you're dead! Heh-heh-heh. *[SONNY slowly raises his hands]*

MA. Are you all right, son?

SONNY. I feel a speech coming on.

MA. Then get it out of your system.

SONNY. *[Stands]* My friends, let me have your attention, please.

GIRLS. Speech! Speech!

MA. Ssssssssh.

SONNY. Thank you, Mother. *[To others]* My friends, we have a grim mystery on our hands.

GIRLS. How soon do we eat?

What's for lunch?

I'm hungry.

Bring on the food.

Let's chow down.

SONNY. Quiet! Our mystery has nothing to do with food. We are concerned with the identity of the person or persons who killed that ... *[His voice breaks]* ... That little dancing divinity.

COLONEL. *[To Lydia]* Divinity. *[He pokes his elbow into her ribs]* That's sugar candy.

LYDIA. *[Angrily]* I know what divinity is. And quit poking me.

COLONEL. Sorry.

SONNY. Someone sitting in this restaurant killed little Cora. *[Pause as he looks from face to face]* Will the guilty party or parties please stand up?

MA. *[Tugging at his sleeve]* The killer isn't going to admit it; that's contrary to human nature.

COLONEL. She's right, Sonny boy. Listen to your mama.

SONNY. *[Ignores Colonel; walks over to platform]* Then suppose I conduct this investigation as though it were an audition.

GIRLS. Five, six, seven, eight. Cuckoo! Cuckoo!

SONNY. If you girls feel that way, suppose you all step up on the platform.

GIRLS. *[As they get on platform]* He's lost his mind.

This is crazy.

I didn't do it.

Let's eat.

What a dummy.

SONNY. Quiet!

GIRLS. Boooooooooooo!

SONNY. *[To audience]* They're not supposed to boo me; I'm not the villain. *[To Girls]* Now speak up, one at a time.

MONDAY. I hated Cora because of her dancing ability, but I didn't kill her.

WEDNESDAY. She was prettier than me, but I didn't shoot her.

FRIDAY. I flat out didn't like her style, but I wouldn't murder her for that reason.

SONNY. *[Walking around]* You all admit that you had a motive for killing her, yet you all deny snuffing out her life.

GIRLS. Yes!

SONNY. On the other hand . . . *[pause]* . . . all you girls own a hand-gun and know how to use same.

COLONEL. *[Jumps to his feet]* I protest the way you are accusing my girls of murder.

SONNY. Sir, no one, least of all I, has accused these . . . uh . . . girls . . . of any crime.

COLONEL. Let the record show that I protested.

SONNY. There is no record. Besides, you'll get your "day in court" very soon.

COLONEL. What's that supposed to mean?

SONNY. Only that you haven't stepped up on the platform yet.

COLONEL. I wouldn't dream of upstaging my girls.

GIRLS. Are you through with us?

    Can we go now?

    I'm hungry.

    Told you all I know.

    We're innocent. *[GIRLS return to their seats at table Up Right]*

SONNY. Colonel, you're next.

COLONEL. Meaning you want me to mount the platform.

SONNY. That's exactly what I mean.

COLONEL. I'll have no truck with this ridiculous kangaroo court.

SONNY. Yet you claim to be innocent.

COLONEL. Of course.

SONNY. Then you have nothing to fear.

COLONEL. Well, since you put it that way.

SONNY. Exactly.

COLONEL. But just for a few minutes. *[He crosses to platform]* I'm here. Are you satisfied?

SONNY. *[Walks around confidently during the time he is interrogating someone]* Maybe yes, maybe no.

COLONEL. What's that supposed to mean?

SONNY. Colonel, I believe you were in your room when the fatal shot was fired.

COLONEL. That absolves me. *[Starts to step down]*

SONNY. Hold it one minute.

COLONEL. I don't have time for this s—

SONNY. You were in your room when the shot was fired.

COLONEL. You're repeating yourself, buster.

SONNY. Was anyone with you?

COLONEL. No.

SONNY. Did anyone see you?

COLONEL. In the total eclipse? *[Laughs]*

SONNY. Did you have any motive for extinguishing the life of the deceased?

COLONEL. Not that I know of.

SONNY. But she did repulse your advances.

COLONEL. Oh . . . in a way . . .

SONNY. You took revenge, because she made you lose face.

MA. *[To audience]* You call that a face?

COLONEL. Listen, kid, I'm not in the habit of being repulsed.

SONNY. So you struck back at her, like the villain you are.

COLONEL. I've had about enough of this monkey business. *[Starts to leave platform]*

SONNY. Not so fast, sir, there are a few more questions . . .

COLONEL. I'm through answering your stupid questions.

SONNY. Begging your pardon, but you sound like a guilty man to me.

COLONEL. That's your opinion. *[Crosses to table where Lydia is sitting and joins her]*

SONNY. *[Crosses to Colonel]* I have another opinion . . . You wanted to get Cora out of the picture because your ex-paramour turned up unexpectedly . . . and you were torn between two women.

COLONEL. Nonsense.

LYDIA. *[Jumps to her feet and accuses Colonel]* The young man is right. You were carrying on a love affair with Cora . . . and I was a threat to your situation. *[LYDIA strides to platform]* Ask me any questions you want to, Sonny. I've got nothing to hide.

SONNY. Thank you. *[Pause]* You say you had every reason to kill her, but you didn't. Why not?

LYDIA. The most elementary reason in the world.

SONNY. And that is . . .

LYDIA. I don't have a gun.

COLONEL. What about the one I gave you?

LYDIA. 'Way back in Sacramento?

COLONEL. It was a birthday present.

LYDIA. I pawned it in Sutter's Mill for money to pay my stagecoach fare . . . *[looks around, frowning]* . . . to this forsaken dump.

MA. *[Jumps to her feet angrily]* Don't call this dump a dump. We serve good food—when we can afford to buy provisions.

LYDIA. Is everybody broke around here? *[Returns to her seat]*

MA. My late husband and his late partner were supposed to know the location of the Lost Frenchman Mine . . . a million dollars in gold.

COLONEL. What do you mean "they were supposed to know"?

MA. They mined it once—then my husband left and couldn't find it again. Now, alas, they are dead and buried. And the secret died with them.

COLONEL. *[To audience]* Curses. Fooled again.

MA. Sonny, is it my turn to step up on the platform?

SONNY. Not unless you want to.

MA. That would be the democratic thing to do. *[Stands up and walks to the platform, then happens to glance down; she is in her stocking feet]* Oh, Son, would you do me a favor?

SONNY. What?

MA. Please get my shoes from under the table.

SONNY. Certainly, Mother. *[He crosses to Down Left table and gets her shoes]*

MA. He's such an obliging son, don't you agree?

COLONEL. He's wonderful, but can he earn a living?

SONNY. Mother, you need new soles for these shoes. *[He removes the envelope. It has been opened]*

COLONEL. You're talking about a pair of women's shoes when the purpose of this inquisition is to find out who slew the little hoofer.

SONNY. I'm getting to that, sir!

COLONEL. *[Mocking him]* "I'm getting to that, sir."

SONNY. As I was saying, Mother, when I picked up your shoes, I noticed that there was an empty envelope in your right shoe. *[Holds up the envelope]*

MA. That's the one that needs re-soling worst.

SONNY. Correct. *[Pause]* Now let me ask you this, was this envelope empty when you first placed it in your shoe?

MA. Well . . . no . . .

SONNY. It was sealed and it contained a letter or other material or both.

MA. That's right.

SONNY. Did you open the envelope?

MA. No . . .

SONNY. Then how did you know what it contained?

MA. The envelope must have been rubbed open by the natural friction of my foot . . . I guess.

SONNY. However it happened, the envelope opened itself?

MA. That's right.

SONNY. When did you read the contents of the envelope?

MA. When I changed— *[flustered]* What makes you think I read the contents?

SONNY. Natural curiosity. The average person would read anything that fell out of a supposedly sealed envelope.

MA. Absolutely, son. I'm just an average person and I do average things. Can I get down from the platform now? This height is making me dizzy.

SONNY. I'll be through shortly.

MA. Please hurry before I faint.

SONNY. You're not dizzy and you're not going to faint. You're a tough old gal.

MA. I hope you meant that as a compliment.

SONNY. *[Hostilely]* What did you read in that letter that made you shoot Cora?!

MA. How . . . how . . . dare you talk to your mother in that tone.

SONNY. I'm going to find out who killed my betrothed, and I don't care where the blame falls.

MA. I don't either, as long as it don't fall on me.

SONNY. Listen closely, Mother, and tell me whether I'm right. You read that letter and there was something in it that drove you to . . . *[his voice breaks]* . . . kill the girl I love.

ALL. Ridiculous.

Preposterous.

His own mother.

Unbelievable.

He must be crazy.

I don't believe it.

MA. Son, I'm surprised at you . . . I can't believe you'd say such things . . .

SONNY. Let's look at the facts. You're desperately in need of money. Your late husband and Cora's father were gold-mining partners. Suppose the contents of this envelope bequeathed the hidden gold to Cora instead of to you . . . *[pause]*

MA. Go on.

SONNY. So you located Pa's old gun and . . . shot Cora dead.

MA. You're overlooking one fact, son.

SONNY. Which is . . .

MA. . . . that I've still got the gun. *[She pulls pistol from under her apron and waves it around. Everybody freezes as she backs out of door Left]*

SONNY. Colonel! Miss Lydia! Don't let my poor misguided mother get away. She may do something rash. Follow her! *[COLONEL and LYDIA run out Left]*

MONDAY. What about us?

WEDNESDAY. We want to save your mother.

FRIDAY. We like her cooking.

SONNY. The back door. *[Points to door Right]* Check the alleys.

GIRLS. We'll find her! *[They run out Right]*

SONNY. *[Looks around to see if he's alone. Then he whispers]* Cora.

CORA. *[Slowly sits up and stretches]* Yes?

SONNY. Are you all right?

CORA. A little stiff, that's all.

SONNY. *[Hurries to her and helps her to her feet]* Our little scheme is working. *[They embrace]*

CORA. You told me your father's gun was loaded with blanks. Thank goodness you were right.

SONNY. *[Seriously]* As we go through life together, my love, you will find that I am *always* right.

CORA. Yes, dear. *[To audience]* I've got news for him. *[KNOCK-ING on door Left]*

SONNY. Quick. Play dead.

CORA. Do I have to, Sonny? *[KNOCKING is repeated]*

SONNY. As soon as we get our hands on the Lost Frenchman Mine map, you can come back to life.

CORA. Lying here makes me sleepy.

SONNY. Then go to sleep. But don't snore. *[She lies down on edge

of platform, and he covers her with tablecloth. KNOCKING repeated]
It's open. Come in. *[The two BUMPKINS enter, shoving and hitting each other]* The auditions are over.

BUMPKINS. Awwwwwwwww. *[Exit Left]*

CORA. *[Whisper]* Are they gone?

SONNY. Yes, but don't get up yet. *[He crosses to door Left and looks out]* Ooooops, here comes Mother. *[MA enters from Left with her hands over her head. She is followed by COLONEL and LYDIA, the former holding a gun on Ma]*

COLONEL. We found her hiding in the stagecoach office.

MA. I'm innocent, Son, I tell you I'm innocent.

SONNY. Then why did you run away?

MA. My mind told me to.

COLONEL. Nonsense.

MA. You've got to believe your old mother, Sonny. I'm innocent. Ask me any question you want to.

SONNY. Where's the map to the Lost Frenchman Mine?

MA. He has it!

COLONEL. She has it!   *[Simultaneously, pointing at each other]*

LYDIA. They have it!

MA. The Colonel promised to marry me if I'd shoot Cora and give him the map to the mine.

LYDIA. So! All your talk of marrying *me* was just a tissue of lies!

COLONEL. Let me explain, sweetheart. I *hypnotized* Mrs. Cleanlivin to say and do all this.

SONNY. *[To audience]* It's called post-hypnotic suggestion. *[He puts his arm around Ma and pulls her to his side]* You're all right now, Mother. Cora and I are going to take good care of you.

MA. Cora . . .?

SONNY. *[To Colonel]* Speaking for the Cleanlivin family and my bride-to-be, I demand you hand over that map. Now!

COLONEL. Have you gone daft? Your bride-to-be-that-ain't lies stone cold dead on yon platform.

CORA. *[Tossing back the tablecloth and springing to her feet]* I am not stone cold dead! Cora Sline lives! *[MA and LYDIA faint; CORA attends to them]*

SONNY. Are you going to hand over that map, or do I have to trounce you good and proper?

COLONEL. Silly boy. *[He points gun at Sonny]*

SONNY. Don't do anything I'll regret.

COLONEL. *[Grabs Cora by the waist and starts to back out door Left. Holds her as a shield]* I'm leaving with two prizes.

CORA. Save me! Save me! *[To audience]* Save the map.

SONNY. Unhand them both, you dirty, dastardly dog.

COLONEL. Try and make me.

CORA. *[To audience]* "Try *to* make me."

SONNY. This is the moment I've been living for. *[He leaps at the COLONEL and they struggle over the gun. CORA steps aside and holds her eyes. The struggle continues. LYDIA slowly gets to her feet. The gun goes off and she grabs her stomach. SONNY wrests the gun from Colonel]*

LYDIA. You got me. *[Feebly]* Help me . . . I'm dying. Call Dr. Jakey. *[She staggers out nearest door]*

COLONEL. Good riddance of bad acting. Heh-heh-heh.

MA. You despicable cad. *[She rises and slaps the Colonel]*

SONNY. *[Holding gun on Colonel]* Mother, call the sheriff. Tell him we've got a murderer with three witnesses.

MA. I won't be a minute. *[Runs out Left]*

CORA. *[Putting her arms around Sonny]* My hero!

SONNY. *[Still holding gun on Colonel]* See if the map is in his coat pocket.

COLONEL. Listen, kids, I've always liked you . . . admired your talents . . . let's make a deal. The wheel of fortune can spin your password to riches.

SONNY. No deals, villain, you're going to the gallows where you so rightly belong. *So shut up.*

CORA. *[Taking map out of Colonel's pocket and giving it to Sonny]* Our passport to a rich, full life.

SONNY. And happiness. Let us not forget happiness.

MA. *[Runs in; breathless]* Sheriff's out of town!

COLONEL. Mrs. Cleanlivin, let's make a deal.

MA. You cad. *[Slaps him. SONNY pokes gun into Colonel's stomach]*

SONNY. Didn't I tell you to shut up!

COLONEL. I believe you did. *[ALL freeze. They hold for about five beats]*

CORA. We can't stand here all day.

SONNY. *[To Ma]* When will the sheriff be back?

MA. Let me catch my breath. *[Gasps for air]* Two deputies are on the way over. *[The two BUMPKINS enter and stand near door Left, covertly nudging and punching each other]*

SONNY. Officers, here's your murderer. Take him away. *[BUMP-KINS grab COLONEL and march him out Left; he protests all the way out, attempting to swing watch fob]*

COLONEL. I'm innocent, I'm innocent, you've got the wrong . . .

MA. This is the proudest moment of my life. *[She puts her arms around Sonny and Cora]*

SONNY. *[Holding up map]* We've got the map, too!

CORA. Give it to your mother, Sonny.

SONNY. But . . . but . . .

CORA. Give it to her. Now.

SONNY. This map is worth a million dollars. *[Gives map to Ma]*

CORA. I care not for riches. Cora Sline was born to dance! *[She goes into a bit of a dance and SONNY joins her as CURTAIN closes]*

The End

PRODUCTION NOTES

Properties

Large carpetbag—Sonny
Sign reading: "Dancers Wanted—Apply Within"—in Sonny's carpetbag
3 Straw suitcases and/or small handbags—Monday, Wednesday, Friday
Watch fob—Colonel
3 Pistols—Monday, Wednesday, Friday
Small carpetbag—Finney
Dainty handbag—Cora
Envelope (#10 manila)—Finney
Large pistol—Colonel
Red checkered napkin—tied around Monday's neck
Toothpick—Wednesday

Costumes and Make-Up

Gay Nineties costumes are recommended. **Col. Quantrell** wears black through-out; **Sonny** may wear white (with a black armband for mourning). **Monday, Wednesday,** and **Friday** are overdressed and tacky, with make-up and hair-dos to match. **Lydia** is also overdressed and over-painted, but more flamboyantly than the triplets, who are rather drab, uncouth, and blah. **Cora** wears tutus throughout—perhaps pink at her first entrance and black later (for mourning).

The Set

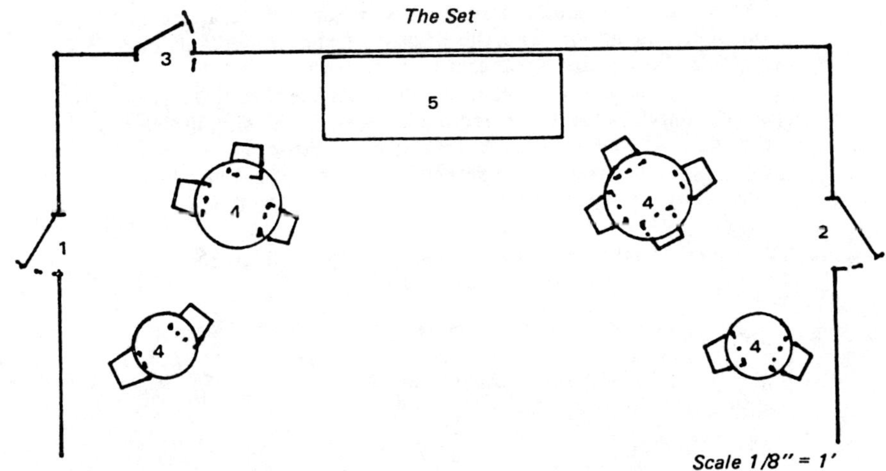

1—Door Right to kitchen
2—Door Left to street
3—Door Up Right to living quarters
4—Four tables with tablecloths and limited table settings, chairs
5—Raised platform against upstage wall

MRS. WIGGS OF THE CABBAGE PATCH

Or, A Page from the Book of Life

A Heart-Rending Melodrama in 3 Acts by Tim Kelly

The famous old story about good-hearted, hard-working Mrs. Wiggs and her beloved cabbage patch has been turned into an old-fashioned melodrama by America's Melodrama Master, Tim Kelly.

"Sometimes I think I'm too good to be true," says Mrs. Wiggs as she goes about spreading sunshine to the appreciation of her neighbors and the disgust of snarling villains like Aristotle Flint, the meanest man in town, and Serafina Crumm, his partner in treachery. But can she save the unsuspecting heiress, Miss Lucy, from Flint's evil? Will she discover Serafina's wicked scheme before it's too late? Will she save young Richard from the lure of the bottle? Will love bloom in the Cabbage Patch—or only cabbages?

A fast-paced laugh-a-minute comedy, easy to stage and a delight for all groups and all audiences.

5 men, 10 women, extras if desired. One simple interior set

Order from

I. E. CLARK PUBLICATIONS
PO Box 246, Schulenburg, TX 78956-0246
Phone (979)743-3232 ** FAX (979)743-4765
E-mail: ieclark@cvtv.net

THE SAGA OF SAGEBRUSH SAL

Wild-West Melodrama in 2 Acts

Here is all the fun that an old-fashioned comic melodrama should have—but with refreshing differences. This one tells the story of sexy Sagebrush Sal, who decides to take over the busiest establishment in town, the Bloody Turnip Saloon. Jake the Snake, its owner, doesn't like the idea, but when Sal kills all his customers with one bullet, Jake snakes out. In the meantime, Sal's delectable, oversized, man-crazy daughter Hazeltine has her troubles with the world's shyest white-hat hero, Heartbleed Haymeadow. The audience laughs so much, you can hardly get on with the show.

"Our mayor played the 'Chief,' a bank vice president was 'Heartbleed,' the City Manager was an Indian . . . Our whole club is still walking on air over the success."—Epsilon Sigma Alpha, Burnet, Texas.

8 males, 9 females, plus extras. Simple set and costumes. 45 minutes to 90 minutes depending on the amount of singing, dancing, olios, entr'actes. Playbook, Director's Production Script, and production rights are available from the publisher.

I. E. CLARK PUBLICATIONS
PO Box 246
Schulenburg, TX 78956-0246
Phone (979) 743-3232 ** FAX (979) 743-4765

MUCH ADO ABOUT MURDER

A 2-Act Audience-Participation Murder Mystery by Pat Cook

The audience gets to play detective in this puzzling, suspenseful murder mystery.

Rich but rotten Carlton Larraby enjoyed punctuating the lives of his family and associates with macabre little surprises. His latest party joke is a Halloween affair with everybody dressed like a character from Shakespeare. But this time the joke is on Carlton—he is gruesomely bludgeoned to death in his study.

During the intermission, the audience is invited to inspect the clue-rich murder room. And then, near the end of the play, each character steps to the front of the stage to answer questions from the audience. "What made this gimmick fun," a newspaper critic commented, "was watching the actors try to stay in character as they improvised answers to questions thrown at them." William Albright, the Houston Post critic, had other compliments:

"Light-hearted fun." "Art shmart . . . theaters can have all the contests and festivals they want, looking for 'serious' plays about the world after the bomb drops and who knows what all. It's . . . audience-pleasing frippery like *Much Ado About Murder* that has 'legs' and will be staged by community, college, amateur, and perhaps even professional theaters from here to Kokomo. After all, Larry Shue's *The Foreigner* is every bit as silly, and has been an off-Broadway hit for . . . years."

5 men, 5 women. Interior set.

I. E. CLARK PUBLICATIONS
PO Box 246, Schulenburg, TX 78956-0246
Phone (979)743-3232 ** FAX (979)743-4765
E-mail: ieclark@cvtv.net